The Ultimate Job Interview Framework

Jeff Altman, The Big Game Hunter*

*TM, The Big Game Hunter, Inc, Asheville, NC 2006

Introduction

The skills needed to find a job are different than the skills needed to do a job. Most job hunters know what they do and they can regurgitate information about it but there's more to getting hired than just that.

One of the things I always tell people I coach is that great athletes all practice. LeBron James practices seven days a week during the season and great entertainers all rehearse. But job hunters tend to go on interviews and the first time the words ever come out of their mouth is when they're asked a question and then wonder why they didn't perform well?

They've never rehearsed their lines with the result being you know they learn the hard way that winging it doesn't work very often. Learning by trial and error makes you miss out on opportunities you could have otherwise had if only you had practiced, if only you practiced the right answers to questions, if only you knew how to interview the right way. But you don't yet have the skills to do it in an interview.

Understand I am differentiating between having the skill set or experience or whatever needed to do the job and communicating that in a way that people interviewing you will receive it much better than they do now. Usually, that's where people have trouble in interviews.

Even if you are hired, the job offer may be for less money than you deserve, all because you made the mistake of thinking you knew how to interview. I can't help you be better at what you do but I can provide you with a formula, with the framework that, if you practice it, will help you outperform almost everyone you compete with for the job.

Learning how to interview in this way will help you demonstrate your knowledge better than most others so that the interviewer will receive it well, believe in you, and trust you.

Congratulations on being wise enough to know you need help.

About Jeff Altman, The Big Game Hunter

I started work as a recruiter back in The Stone Ages, not quite when dinosaurs roamed the earth, but it was 1972 when I first got into search. Please don't hold it against me that I worked as a recruiter. I wasn't one of the bad guys who gave the field a bad reputation.

If you look at my LinkedIn profile, you'll see I've received thousands of endorsements and recommendations from my time doing recruiting. I'm proud of that because we all know that everyone hates recruiters . . . But they liked my work.

As I gained experience, I began to pay attention to what my clients were telling me and what the job hunters I was representing were telling me as part of the debrief after interviews. I started to think of how could we do it better than just simply looking at the job description sending them out to with little more advice than simply, "give a firm handshake and maintain eye contact so that I earn a fee."

Back in 1972, headhunting wasn't much different than that. I started to think of ways where I could help people get hired and, in doing that, I started to break down, how someone could do it better, how they could do it differently, and advantage themselves in the search. That's where I started to evolve this framework.

Now, I host, No BS Job Search Advice Radio, the #1 podcast in Apple Podcasts for job search which will celebrate its 10th anniversary and 2000th episode in November 2020. My YouTube channel at JobSearchTV.com has been rated a Top 10 channel for job search.

In addition, you can watch me on the Job Search TV app for Amazon products and Roku and through BingeNetworks.tv for Apple TV and 90+ smart sets worldwide.

This is the first book I've written and more than six years. I've written eight before that and discontinued the first six recently because they became dated.

It became time for me to share something important, cultivate over many years to help you land your next job.

Table of Contents

What Every Employer Assesses for When They Hire

What does a company want to find out about you when they interview you? What are they trying to find out when they evaluate and assess you? In most cases, hiring staff or temporary workers starts with a job description. Someone sat down and consciously thought of what skills and experience they needed on their staff.

But the truth of the matter is that most job descriptions are 80% accurate. That's because no one writes them from scratch anymore when a position opens up. Someone resigns in a hiring manager calls over to HR on a Friday afternoon and asks, "Do you have the job description that we use the higher Jeff?" "Yes, I can find it."

"Great. He just gave notice that I need a replacement. Can you get out to our vendors and other resources, posted on the website and elsewhere, and see who you get onto my calendar for next Tuesday or Wednesday?"

No one ever updates them. They just don't have the time. Besides, hiring managers think that HR has nothing better to do than to cater to them so if the job descriptions a little bit off and HR has its time wasted and wastes the time of third-party recruiters, they don't care. They just want to start seeing people and doing it as quickly as possible.

When a manager starts to interview, when they point to someone on their team and asked them to interview, hopefully, they start by assessing for competence. I say "hopefully" because so many people report that they work with incompetent colleagues. Hopefully, an employer has developed a series of questions that help them evaluate and assess skills competency for the skills that are needed. In reality, many of them just simply wing it during their interviews asking random and arbitrary questions to evaluate a person's knowledge.

But skills competency is only one element of what a company is evaluating. These all fall into the category of soft skills—hard to assess for qualities that differentiate one person from another.

Companies also look for chemistry. How do you fit into the firm and its corporate culture? This soft skill is derived from the interviewer's interpretation of how you will fit into the organization and how well you will work with your colleagues.

The problem with that is both you and they, are on good behavior. When I started in recruiting it didn't take me long to figure out the job hunters were on good behavior. But it took me a while to figure out that my institutional customers were on good behavior, too. I realized that when it popped into my mind that I never heard of an employer say to one of my candidates, "You know, I've got a problem. I've taken over this group and have a bunch of losers in here. We have a lot of work to do and no one capable enough to do it. My predecessor was fired and so was hers. It doesn't take a genius to realize that unless I turn this thing around, I'm next."

Instead, they all have these happy faces on, talking about interesting work in a wonderful team of people. "That I mentioned were like family around here?" Sure. The families in all the US holiday movies that hate one another and want to kill one another whenever they get together. No one discloses that kind of family.

The next quality that they evaluate for is character. Do you have character? Are you a character? Both? Most companies require character from their employees. Some jobs demand that a person be a character, too!

Self-Confidence is next. How does your behavior inspire confidence that you are the solution to the problem and not someone else's problem? Self-confident people ALWAYS do better than nervous frightened people

The last quality in the formula they try to determine is whether you have charisma. Charismatic people always do better on interviews than non-charismatic individuals. When you think of the importance of charisma, you can think of individual politicians, business leaders, and entertainers who all possessed that certain quality when they walked into a room, on stage, or on the screen that you are watching. They possess that certain quality that makes them stand out and others look small. Although it is not a requirement, employers tend to like hiring charismatic people.

These qualities—competence, self-confidence, charisma, chemistry, and character—all add up to a company, a hiring manager choosing someone that they trust.

If you are interviewing for a leadership role, it's not like someone is going to ask you: "Are you a leader." Yeah, I'm a leader." "Good. That was the right answer."

Every question is going to have a macro and micro component to it. The micro is going to be the specific answer to the question you are asked. The macro, the big picture, will be how your manner and behavior congruent (or not) with their image of someone in the job. Your mannerisms are observed; your behavior is scrutinized to see how you "fit" the job, too.

Is It the Resume or My Interviewing That's Keeping Me from Getting Hired?
A. Yes.

Your resume may be keeping you from getting hired. Been interviewing may be why you're not getting hired. A LinkedIn profile that doesn't draw people to you or is incongruent with your resume may be why you're not getting hired. This is a puzzle with thousands of pieces.

If someone isn't getting interviews, usually it's the resume that's the problem. It may be generic and may not make a case for someone fitting the job it's available. It and the LinkedIn profile may be incongruent. One may emphasize one skill or experience while the other one emphasizes a different one.

Once you've received the invitation, if you can't get past the screener (company recruiter), you don't do phone interviews well. If you're getting past the screener to the next step and nothing is happening further, there's a disconnect either with the person who's there to evaluate your skills or with a hiring manager.

Usually at this stage, what a firm is looking for is skills competence and they want to trust the person that they hire. So, there's an emotional component to it that most job hunters don't address in the interview. As a result, they conduct themselves in the interview as though all they need to do is recite facts of their experience.

They think of themselves, "I just have to recite this stuff and demonstrate to them that I know it and that's enough to get hired. Thus, to me, once it's past the resume, once you're starting the conversations, more than two-thirds of the breakdown can be attributed to interview skills.

The statistics show that most people think that they are above average at interviewing. That means that some people are above the midpoint, summer at the midpoint and many are below it. Statistically, that means most of you are poor to middling at best.

As a result, just like any great athlete, entertainer, and public speaker will improve with practice, so can you. Practice is the most important differentiator (after skills) between candidates.

Winning Interviews Begins Before the Interview

1. Prepare for the Screener to Contact You

No matter whether you've applied for a job or been contacted by a firm, your first point of contact with this organization is designed to superficially screen you for the role. On occasion, a hiring manager will call. Typically, it is someone who will do a superficial screening about your background.

Typically, they will introduce themselves and ask questions about your work. They don't have in-depth knowledge about your area of expertise. What they are listening for is whether you have done the things previously that they need you to do now. They also want to make sure that you can communicate well and have a job history that doesn't scare them.

Often their questions sound something like, "Have you done this?" "Have you done that?"

"Tell me about what you did."

Do you remember what I said earlier?

If you have seen a job description, it's 80% accurate. You don't know which part is inaccurate. You don't know with certainty what the emphasis is in the job description.

If you haven't seen a job description, you are flying blind. You have no idea what they are actually looking for.

As a result, they have all the power because they have the knowledge and you have none of it. Your goal is to level the playing field so that you understand what they are going to be evaluating you for.

As a result, you have to ask what I call "the single best question to ask on an interview." In fact, it **Is** the single most important question to ask on any interview.

When the screener reaches out to you and gets you on the phone, you first have to decide whether you are mentally prepared to speak with them.

If not, respond by saying, "Thanks for reaching out to me. I'm in with some people (or an on the place where I have a good signal or some other excuse).

"Would it be possible for me to call you back at . . ." Suggest a time where you can return the call.

Too often, when people are mentally unprepared for an interview, they become accommodating to the caller. Unfortunately, they don't perform as well as they might otherwise. You're always better off at a time when you can perform at a high level. You only have one chance with the screener.

If they reached out to you by email or LinkedIn's inMail to set up a conversation, schedule the conversation, however, make the point of saying, "Please forward a job description to me. If the job you have open is something, I'm neither qualified to do or interested in, let's save us both some time." If this is a third-party recruiter, they may tell you they don't have a job description. "My client spoke to me about this. I have some rough notes but I don't have a formal job description."

Respond by saying, "walk me through the job, please."

Now, we are up to the question you have to be prepared to ask in the first contact.

Let's say they call you on the phone. They will probably confirm that it's you.

"Is this Jeff?"

"Hi! This is Rona Recruiter from Make Up the Name of a Company. Is this still a good time to speak?"

"Thanks so much for making time to reach out to me." Assuming you've never seen a job description, you start by saying, *Thanks so much for making time to speak with me. Would you tell me about the job as you see it and what I can do to help?*" Usually, the format of an interview starts with them asking you to answer the question, "Tell me about yourself," or, "Walk me through your background, please." Then you do. For a while, they follow up with questions to go into more detail. The conversation evolves to a point where they begin to ask behavioral interview questions.

"Tell me about a time when you . . . "

"Explain a situation where you had to . . . "And you do.

Eventually, it gets to a point where they ask you, "So, do you have any questions for us?"

You respond by asking, "Tell me about the job." They tell you about the job.

You say, "Sounds terrific!"

"Great. We'll get back to you."

The problem is that by the time you've heard about the job, it's too late to do anything with that information. They've already decided whether or not to bring you back even if they're not telling you at that time.

If you're a more experienced individual, I want you to ask one additional question:

"What would you say the two or three biggest challenges with are that I would have to face?" By asking that question at the beginning, you understand what it is that they're looking for at the beginning of the interview so that you can talk about what you've done that matters to them and not just talk about what you've done.

You now have the roadmap for what they want. You know the job description as they are currently thinking about it which may be different than the one that you've received.

In addition, you also know about the challenges ahead of you if you're a more experienced individual (Usually, a company will not tell you the truth about the challenges when you are more junior.

Rather than put them in the position of lying to you, I would rather skip the question rather than put them in the position where they can lie to you).

2. Interview Do's

Treat everyone you speak to with respect. Their opinions of you might be solicited during hiring decisions (or, if you were particularly rude, they will seek someone out to share their opinion).

There was a time where I was trying to hire someone from my firm. After meeting with her and a few of the salespeople, I asked my receptionist for an opinion.

"I would have been treated more nicely if our case of athlete's foot. She was so rude to me." Suffice it to say we didn't hire this person.

On Wall Street, one of the most important people in the interview process for one firm used to be "the shoeshine guy." This African-American man had been quietly going about his work for years shining the broker shoes. His instincts about people were considered beyond world-class.

Treating this person badly or indifferently was grounds for being rejected for a position. Yet some people look down on this man who had done nothing wrong to them and treated him as though he were lower-class. To the people in this organization, he was class.

Listen to be sure you understand your interviewer's name and the correct pronunciation.

If you are not sure how to pronounce someone's name, before you say it, ask him/her to pronounce it for you. I know many people born outside of the United States are very gracious with the mispronunciation of their name. They explain it away rather than be rude. That doesn't permit you to mispronounce their name. If anything, the question about correct pronunciation earns you points.

Maintain good eye contact during the interview whether in-person or video. If you are on camera, line it up so that you are making eye contact. Look for something along the lines of, "Speaker View." If you're meeting someone in person, don't stare so intently that you look like a psychopath. I've interview people like that. I remember feeling like I wanted to make sure that they didn't have any weapons with them!

Respond to questions and back up your statements about yourself with specific examples whenever possible. Ask for clarification if you don't understand a question.

Be thorough in your responses, while being concise in your wording. With very few exceptions, your answers should last no longer than one minute and 15 seconds. If you take longer than that, you risk losing their attention and concentration. We live in a culture that has a short attention span. Taking longer than that causes their mind to drift off to the next meeting, lunch, A call they are supposed to make, and a variety of other distractions.

Demonstrate a positive attitude. The interviewer is evaluating you as a potential subordinate, coworker, or hire. Behave like someone you would want to work with. Few people want to hire someone who is hypercritical, negative, or just a plain downer. How many of those people if you enjoyed working with? They are no different

Have great questions prepared to ask the interviewer. I will offer a few later on, as well as a question that will let you know what the next steps will be.

When the interviewer concludes an in-person interview, offer a firm handshake (assuming social distancing is not the rule of the day), and make eye contact as you shake their hands. Tell them that you appreciate them making time to meet with you and that you're looking forward to the next steps in the process because you're very interested if that's true. If it isn't true just thank them for making time to meet with you.

After the interview, make notes right away so you don't forget any details or questions. I remember debriefing candidates who been on multiple interviews and had gotten confused about who said what to them. Save yourself some heartache by just taking a few quick notes.

Email or text a thank-you message to the interviewer promptly. Have someone proofread it before it is sent. In the case of a tie, hiring managers sometimes use perceived interest as a tiebreaker.

3. INTERVIEW DON'TS

Don't make negative comments about previous employers, professors, or others. Hiring managers think that when you leave them, as inevitably you will, you will describe them that way, too.

Don't falsify application materials or answers to interview questions. First of all, it's wrong. Secondly, if you are caught falsifying information on an application, it is grounds for being fired. Third, it is much too easy to be caught given how much data is available to employers and recruiters. I remember talking to someone and looking at their resume and looking at the information that they had inputted into my applicant tracking system. Two jobs had disappeared. "What happened to . . . "I mentioned the name of the firm. Silence. "And so and-so?" Silence. I made my point.

Don't give the impression you are only interested in your starting salary. Money is important to me and it is to you, too. Employers like to hire people who are interested in their opportunity and working for their company.

Don't act as though you would take any job or are desperate for employment. Acting desperate is just as undesirable in job search, as it is in dating.

Don't go to extremes with your posture like slouching or sitting rigidly on the edge of your chair.

Don't chew gum, smell like smoke, or wear cologne or perfume. Some people, like my wife, have sensitivities to smells.

Turn off your cell phone or set it on vibrate. If you forget to and it rings, do not take the call. Don't look at or respond to texts. There are many stories that HR professionals share about the person that they are interviewing taking a call during the interview. Although the rules may not seem fair, these are the rules **UNLESS** you warn them at the beginning of the interview about the possibility of needing to take a call. An ill child or the possibility of an imminent passing of a family member are among the few reasons for taking a call.

4. Research the Company and the Person You'll Be Meeting with or Speaking To

You may know what some of the large firms do but not every firm. You may know what that large firm does but not the specific group whose manager you will be speaking with. Be clear about what the role is you'll be interviewing for and where it fits into the organization.

Look up the profile of the person or people you'll be meeting with or speaking to on LinkedIn. Are they in HR? Are they a potential peer? Are they the hiring manager? What is their role within the firm and what do they do?

Remember, a screener may only be looking to check off the boxes of your experience. A peer may want to confirm your knowledge and experience in the course of the interview. After all, you'll be working side-by-side with them and they don't want to be in the position of rescuing you all the time. The hiring manager has the concern about whether you can do the job, whether you are a potential management headache, and, like parents of young children, whether you will reflect well upon them.

Researching the company and the person you'll be meeting with should also be done in several other places.

a) **Google**. Look both up and see whether they have an online history. Certainly, the company will but what about the individual you're talking to? Are they in press releases? Do they speak for the business at conferences? What is their public professional visibility if any?

b) **Wikipedia.** Many larger firms will have detailed articles written about them and the article will include links to other stories written about them.

c) **YouTube**. This is one of the biggest changes that has taken place in the past few years as more and more firms mobilize YouTube to communicate with the public. The hiring manager may have videos about their ideas on YouTube.

d) **LinkedIn**. Your first-level connections are often a great resource for information about the person you'll be speaking with. Maybe, they can introduce you to a second level connection who is even more knowledgeable. Don't hesitate to reach out and ask. They can only say no or ignore your request . . . But they can also say yes!

INTERVIEW MISTAKE: When I started working as a recruiter, sometimes, you needed to go to the library to find out about a company. At times that then, it was permissible to ask an employer about their firm and what it did if no research was available . . . And they knew it, too. Now, there is no reason to ask an interviewer what their company does. It's all online.

5. Meeting the Hiring Manager

In advance of the meeting, practice the opening question(s) again. Now that you're meeting the person that you will be reporting to, tailoring your response to their answer to this question is pivotal.

Also, I want you to prepare three stories that fit STAR, SOAR, or PAR based upon your understanding of the job. Each story, like each answer, should last **no more than 1 minute to 1 minute and 15 seconds.** This is important because we live in a culture with a short attention span. No one listens for very long. If your answers start to run long, they stop paying attention. They start to think about lunch, that phone call they need to return, the next meeting, anything but you.

STAR= Situation or Task, Action, Result (for less experienced people)

SOAR= Situation, Objective, Action, Result (more experienced people)

PAR= Problem, Action, Result (senior leadership)

STAR example: I was given a project by my manager to assist with the development of a new application for the accounting group (situation). My part of the application needed to be coded in (Java, C++, whatever) and needed to be completed within six weeks. So, what I did was . . . (Action). The result was I completed my portion of the project a week early, was able to help one of my colleagues get her work done. The work we did was able to help the firm generate an additional $1.2 million.

SOAR example: I took over a project for my predecessor that was already two weeks behind schedule (situation) but needed to be completed on time because of regulatory requirements (objective). So, what I did was meet with my new team to understand where the breakdown or breakdowns were occurring. I met with the user population to make sure that they understood what was occurring, with their particular needs were and to commit to them that the firm would meet its requirements no matter what. The result was with a lot of effort by a great and committed team of people we were able to get back on track and deliver more than what they asked for as well as what the government required. As a result of this, we were able to help these organizations within our company 8% of the usual expenses and get a big burden off their back with the government.

PAR example: For the last three years, sales were down dramatically for our firm when I took over the function. Our product offerings were not resonating with the market. Our sales leadership and staff were leaving regularly. There was no continuity in our marketing messaging and there were complaints from a few long-time customers about the reliability of our offerings (problem). So, what I did was . . . (Action). As a result of our joint efforts were able to improve sales by 9% in year one, 17% the year two, and 34% in year three, develop a cohesive message for our offerings, involve our clients regularly with our product planning to ensure there was meeting their particular needs (result).

The Theater of Interviewing

Interviewing involves theatre. You're a performer on the stage. I want to be clear when I say "performer," I'm not suggesting liar. The idea is to deliver the lines in a way that the audience will receive it well. That's preface number one.

Preface number two is, most job descriptions if you have one, are about 80 percent accurate. You have to stop and think for yourselves how are most job descriptions created?

What usually happens is that someone gives notice to the hiring manager. Now, the person needs to be replaced. They call her or they call their manager for final authorization and the conversation goes like this, "Chris just gave notice. Do you have that job description we used to hire him? Could you get it out to your sources? Could you get an ad up on LinkedIn or Indeed and see who you can get onto my schedule on Tuesday." No one has ever updated it.

The problem with that the position is more than just a flat documented was at the time it was created. Since then, the job is involved in it will emphasize one thing or another more than it originally did. Additional things are added and removed from it in their thinking so you're not necessarily operating with the best information. You've got most of it or at least got a good part of it, but may be different than at the time they hired Chris.

Judging how most HR professionals respond when I say that 80% of job descriptions are accurate (they laugh), they think it's even less than that.

So, I believe that when you get the first phone call or you're doing the in-person interview, as soon as the phone rings and you recognize it as a recruiter, or as soon as the conversation is about to start in person, it begins with, "Thanks so much for making time to reach out to me." Now, let's work with the assumption that a screener is making the phone call.

Now they will introduce themselves

"I'm Javier from such and such firm."

"Thanks so much for reaching out to me."

If you responded to an ad: "I recall the position description, but I wanted to get your take on the role. Would you tell me about the position as you see it and what I can do to help?"

If you were referred by a third-party recruiter, "Noor described the position to me but I wanted to get your take on the role. Could you tell me about the job as you see it and what I can do to help?"

The same is true if you're talking with the hiring manager for the first time and you've already spoken with HR. "I was interviewed by Ronnie the Recruiter in HR and they describe the position to me but I want to get your take on the role. Could you tell me about the position as you see it and what I can do to help?"

If you are meeting someone in person, you ask this question as you lower your butt into the chair to begin the conversation. You ask it before they have a chance to ask you anything because it is important to know what the target is that they're aiming for in this interview. When you're being interviewed by video, arrived a minute or two early so that you are waiting for them. Once they connect and open the session, after a sentence of two of pleasantries, ask the question.

Asking this question at the beginning accomplishes a few different things.

1. **Because everyone's distracted these days, you're pulling them into the conversation.** So, they now have to tell you what they're looking for, but, more importantly, they're either confirming what's in the job description you have in front of you or what they're doing is cleaning up some of the little details or nuances that are top of mind for them that they're going to want to screen you for. Just as you're in the last few inches of reaching the seat, you want to start the conversation before they have a chance to do it. Just to be clear what often happens is one of a couple of things. Now you know about the job.

2. **If they say, "yeah, we'll get to that later," you've learned something about them.** It doesn't mean you shouldn't pay attention,

but you've learned that they like to play things close to the vest and they're not going to necessarily be forthcoming with you at any point during your interview cycle. I think that's useful to know. Part of what I coach people about is noticing how you connect with the interviewer. If you are going to be dealing with "a detached individual," "a poker player who is hard to read" throughout this who's just going to be there with going through their mental checkboxes, that's all they care about, you will find it difficult to get a read on this person during the interview process and, probably, once you're on board. After all, they are being "cold fish." Withholding. Flat. Again, it is information that helps you manage your expectations.

3. **It eliminates the power differential between the two of you.** After all, in the typical interview, they have all the knowledge of what they are looking for and you have known or little. That gives them a huge advantage throughout the process. Once you know what the target is, you can tailor all of your answers to talk about what

you've done that matters to them instead of just talking about what you've done.

Many people forget that the most important thing in interviewing, like in sales, is the idea of putting yourself in the seat of their needs and not just talking about yourself. They did make the mistake of spending too much time basking in their own magnificence, rather than explaining how they solve the problem that the manager has.

Now, just to be clear, if you just blurt out, "So, what are you looking for, it's not going to work. You won't present as well as if you use my question.

How to Answer "Tell Me About Yourself"

From there, the interview is going to segue into them asking you their habitual opening question of, "Tell me about yourself and what you've been doing professionally," or "walk me through your background." Here's where you are going to combine the typical answer and combine it with the information that you just learned from them.

Start with a 20-second overview of your background. For example, *"I've been in the field for the last 15 years. Most recently I've been working for so and so where I've done this and that and this and that."* Take 15 to 20 seconds giving them an overview of your background. Then, from there you use a bridge phrase that's going to pull them into the conversation.

"But what's probably most relevant about my background for this position is my experience with . . . And then you start feeding back to them your experience that relates to what it is they just told you they were looking for.

By doing this, you've confirmed the basic information that got you the interview.

You've connected the dots for them immediately with your relevant experiences.

Also, you are not making them work to find it out like so many job hunters do.

This is important because, as with your resume and positioning relevant experience earlier in the resume, when you offer it up early in the interview, employers believe that the experience is more current and relevant for what they are looking for.

John had been a client of mine for many years when he decided to change jobs. He came to me

after 17 interviews for advice about what he was doing wrong. We met in my apartment in Greenwich
Village so I could listen to his interview.

I asked him to walk me through his background. I listen to his answer and after two minutes stopped him.

"Is it my imagination," I began, "or are you bored?" He looked surprised.

"You've been on 17 interviews and asked this question 17 times. Many of the other questions are repetitive, too. You sound bored, disinterested, and flat."

"For you, you have been asked this question so many times already but for them, it is opening night for the play and they want to see a great performance."

I continued, "can you imagine what it's like to be a Broadway performer. You work six days a week for eight shows. Every week is the same in every song you sing is the same. For the audience, they have spent a lot of money to see you perform. They don't care that you have been doing this all week long. They want to see a great performance, as good as the one on opening night."

His next three interviews yielded three offers.

Interview Mistakes to Watch Out for:

a) **Talking about what you've done and not talking about what you've done that matters to them.** In the typical interview, job hunters talk about what they've done. Your goal is to talk about what you've done that matters to them and not just what you've done. The difference between the two is that if you talk about what you've done that matters to them, you are telling them about how you can do their job. When you talk about what you've done, you're telling them about your past and much of it may not be relevant to them.

b) **If your answer starts to go on too long, you risk boring them and losing their attention to what you're saying.** Remember, we live in a culture with many distractions. Keeping their attention is critical. Don't bore them by droning on and on and on and on . . . You get my point.

When I answer subsequent questions, I can take more time, right?

In any first conversation, give them the equivalent of an outline so that they can deep dive into the portions of the subcategories. With outlines, there are always subheadings underneath the main topics.

You want them to dig into what they want to dig into rather than do a "soliloquy." You are whetting their appetite for more, rather than anticipating and answering every possible permutation and data point they *might* be interested in.

What happens in the next part of the interview?

Usually, what happens next is they're going to start to want to explore what your background is and what your experiences are and get a clearer sense of what you've accomplished. **This leads to Storytime!** Stories are not just for bedtime. They are for interviewing because we all tend to learn and understand through stories. This is where the stories I asked you to prepare before the interview are brought out and delivered for them.

Remember, you may have heard small differences between what the job description

told you from which you prepared your stories and what the interviewer told you at the beginning of your interview.

It is important to adapt your stories based on the information you've obtained at the beginning of the interview. Otherwise, you will probably be barking up the wrong tree.

As in the movies, you rode in on that horse and rescued the situation. As in all stories, the villagers (the people you helped) lived happily ever after.

Another example of a story might be something along the lines of, "I took over a project from someone who quit suddenly. They were already two months behind and saw the handwriting on the wall. They needed to leave. So, I had to get it back on time quickly because we only had six more weeks to go before, we needed to deliver this thing and were already way behind. So, what I did (notice that we're on to the action already) was meet with the different people in the user population, met with my team, understood where we were, understood what their needs and concerns were, got everyone's buy-in, and then we worked like maniacs to get this done. I delivered it three days early, so we had adequate time to (fill in the blank). The result was we had overjoyed people, writing recommendations for me, talking to my Senior Vice President because I had saved x number of dollars of what over what they feared might happen. The project ultimately helped the firm make y number of dollars.) Now, that's a condensed version that would take about a minute to say to someone.

Reminder: The difference between adequate answers and excellent ones are (1) giving an answer that shows your fit for the role and (2) practice.

Part of practicing your answer is delivering the lines conversationally. Do not sound formal or "professional." Sound as though you are talking to a close friend, your wife, husband, partner, knowledgeable brother, or sister. You wouldn't sound stiff or rigid with them, would you?

In doing a mock interview with someone recently, I asked them to tell me one of their stories. I listen to or answer and then asked her to rate herself.

"I would give myself a five," she said.

"I would rate is 6.5," I told her. "Let's try it again," I suggested.

She was better with her second effort and right yourself a seven. I thought she was a little bit better and told her so. I pointed out that she still sounded,

"professional."

"Talk to your brother."

When she finished this presentation, it was very clear how big a difference she made in her presentation. A definite nine.

We all need an honest critique as much as possible. It isn't that you need to get ripped apart. You need to see how your presentation lands on someone and whether they are convinced by what you say, interested in what you say, and think it would be effective.

Failures are often the result of a lack of preparedness. Practice often enough that it seems like second nature. **Then practice again so it doesn't sound canned and flat.**

When your answer comes across as though you are fumbling around for it, rather than telling you crisply, you are not inspiring confidence that you are the solution to what they're looking for. "Inspiring confidence" is the gut feeling you're trying to generate for them. They trust you. The more you fumble around, the more reluctant they are to surrender their hearts to you and, thus, as you're piecing your answer out, the message you give is, "They are unsure of himself themselves."

Projecting uncertainty is not a demonstration of confidence. Projecting uncertainty comes about as a result of a lack of preparedness and causes them not to believe you.

REMINDER: Don't just simply recite facts. Use your voice to connect with the interviewer. Sell how hard it was to accomplish what you did but you did it despite how difficult it was.

An answer should not be longer than one minute and 15 seconds. The way you do that is by practicing predictable questions that you will be asked on an interview.

Thus, even if they ask you something a little different, you can adapt your prepared story to what they are looking for in the amount of time I'm saying to do it in.

At some point, they're going to ask you if you have any questions for them.

Usually, at this point, you would ask about the job. But since they already told you about it at the beginning of the interview, **you can ask a clarifying question.**

A clarifying question is one where you clear up an issue in your mind that surfaced in the course of their interview.

For example, Ramesh listened to a description of a manager's job but a lot of the questions he was asked were really in the weeds of the work, a lot of coding questions that didn't seem to fit with what you might think a manager might do day-to-day.

To clarify this, he asked, *"When you describe the position to me, you described it as a manager role with a staff of x number of people. But I noticed you asked a lot of coding questions. Would you give me a sense of how much time you would expect someone to be coding versus managing?"*

That is an example of a clarifying question. It clears up any confusion about the nature of the role so that you don't have to let it sit in your mind festering. If there is nothing to clarify at this time, you don't have to ask a question like this.

The next one is a throwaway question that is designed to set up the one that follows. It's also going to make them feel good that you've asked them a question that they can answer.

"Let's say you hire me and I come on board, what are your expectations of me for the first 30, 60, 90 days?"

Now, you'll find they all say the same thing. *"We're going to want you to get acclimated. Get to know everyone. Fit into the environment."* You know it's all about onboarding and helping you feel comfortable. They all know how to answer that question.

The next one is the more important one of the two.

"Let's say you hire me and I come on board. It's a year from now and you are thrilled with the decision you made to hire me. What would I have accomplished during that year that would make you think that way?"

What you're learning from that is how are they going to measure you for success. Every once in a while, you discover their expectations are out of whack. Not asking this question puts you in jeopardy.

Marty took a position running a very large department with an organization. One of his responsibilities was to deliver a major program for the firm. He didn't ask many questions about the program and was surprised to find out when he came on board that 80% of the money had been spent on it and only 20% of the work had been done. He was going to be the fall guy for his new boss!

Had he asked any questions about it and what success would look like for him once he joined, he never would've accepted an offer from them.

REMINDER: Interviewing is a two-way process. You have to be evaluating and assessing them, too, to determine if you should join them. If you spend all of your time trying to make them happy, you are spending zero time getting your questions answered.

Finding out how you're going to be evaluated with the question I'm telling you to ask also sends the signal that you don't just want to do the job and be ordinary. You want to be terrific. So, how are they going to evaluate you? What is success going to look like for you?

I suggest two more questions. They are optional, but I believe you'll see their value.

Could you give me a sense of your timeline for the next steps?

This allows you to manage your expectations about when you're going to hear back.

There are several possible answers. For example, they might say, "Well, I have 24 more people to speak within the next few weeks. I expect will have a decision sometime after hell freezes over." What they are telling you is that you are part of a casting call and they are going to go through the motions of talking to everyone in the hemisphere who might be vaguely qualified before making a decision. Or, they may be unsure about what they're looking for and you haven't convinced him that it's you.

Another possible answer is, "I expect you'll hear from us early part of next week." That one is better but certainly noncommittal. If they said something like that to you, I would respond by asking, "If I haven't heard from you by the latter part of the week, is it okay for me to follow up?"

There are two types of responses that you might get to that question. The first one is, "Sure!" Nothing bad about that one. Occasionally, someone will say, "Wait." The question sounds like pressure to them. Their response was hearing the early part of next week was not sincere.

Sometimes you'll hear them say, "I've got one or two more people to speak with. We should be done by the weekend. By the time everyone on the team gets together, it's Monday afternoon or Tuesday morning."

Then follow-up by asking, "So if I haven't heard from you by Wednesday, would be okay if I followed up?"

In both instances, asking for permission to follow up means that they have okayed it. You are not being one of those "pushy people" that you dread.

The final possible answer you might hear is something that would be similar to, "I expect early next week you get a call from Rona the Recruiter to schedule you for three meetings with people who report to me. Assuming they go well I have

you meet with my boss later part of the week."
Much more committed to pursuing you, aren't
they?

**REMINDER: Everything the employer says
and does is telling you something. What it tells
you will be confirmed by their behavior.**

Once they've told you when you might expect to
hear back, you will have permission to follow up
with them after that. For example, if they tell you,
"I expect you'll be hearing back from us by the
early part of next week," you can follow-up by
asking,

"So, if I haven't heard from you by Wednesday or
Thursday, is it okay if I follow up with you?"
Generally, they will respond in one of two ways.
The first one is, "Sure, follow-up with (me with
Rona the

Recruiter, whoever). The other one is, "WAIT."
There is a message in that word, "wait," that
signals to you that there feeling pressure and that
they don't like it. The reason they feel the pressure
is because they don't care as much about choosing
you as you feel about being chosen.

Assuming that you have permission to follow up
and do so if you don't hear back, follow-up one

more time a few days later. After that, don't chase them anymore. A few things may be going on.

The first one is they are still interviewing. Thus, they're not ready to communicate a decision but don't want to say that to you. The second one, reflecting cowardice, is they don't want to say, "No," to you. They are hoping you go away. If you remember back to what it was like to be dating, when you didn't hear back from someone after a date, you might call them back once and maybe twice before you took the hint. Whether it is an agency recruiter, a corporate recruiter, or the hiring manager, when you don't hear back after multiple phone calls, the statistical probability is that you've been rejected. They don't want to say that to you because they don't want to get into an argument. Sometimes, if they are just not ready to move forward, they will circle back to you when they are.

GREAT! In the meantime, don't be like one of those people who can't take a hint.

Some people wonder why I recommend a second call or email. Sometimes they forget to follow up. Sometimes they never get your voicemail or, when was recorded, it was garbled and they have no idea who called. Also, many of the calls we receive are spam or Robocalls so they never check them anymore. Sometimes your emails may be called by spam filters. There are a million reasons why they never received your message. The second call is an opportunity to try one more time to get through.

THE FINAL QUESTION:

Is there anything that you've heard *or not heard* that gives you a reason to hesitate about my being qualified for this role?

The reason to ask this question is because interviewers aren't always skillful at interviewing people. They may also be distracted or unprepared at the time of the interview and ask questions that lead you one way an answer that went in a different direction.

Not long ago, two men that I coach asked this question. They both heard about things in the answer that told them that something was missing in one of their answers. What they learned was they were asked a question that guided them in one direction but the hiring manager wanted something different. That's because the question asked wasn't as clear as the interviewer thought.

Each responded with, "Oh! When you asked that question about such and such, you were looking for my background with this! Let me tell you about it." They both went on to clarify their experience and were invited back. That never would've happened had they not asked this question

So, the idea is to always ask where they may be reluctant to believe that you are qualified for the role.

Interviews are not just about confirming data. I don't care what industry you are in or what you do in that field. Many competent people can do what you do as well as you. When firms hire, your future boss wants to believe that they can trust you, they that they don't have to worry about you and that you are NOT high maintenance. Thus, when they evaluate people to hire, they are looking for not just competence, but self-confidence, character, chemistry as well as, ideally, charisma. All of which adds up to their trust in you.

Remember, trust is the feeling, not an objective fact. Your smile can go a long way toward giving them that "warm fuzzy" that they want to feel.

Don't forget to try to connect person to person with the interviewer.

Interview Questions to Prepare For

Earlier, I explained how to answer, "Tell me about yourself," or "Walk me through your background.

Here are a few more to prepare for.

1. What is Your Greatest Weakness?

Instead of taking a strength and reframing it as a weakness, try offering a weakness . . . but doing it with style.

The standard way many people are taught to answer this question is to begin pretending to think for a second, break eye contact, look back at the interviewer, and say something like, "Hmm. That's a really good question. What comes to mind is that, sometimes, not often, sometimes, I work too hard. When I do that eventually I wear down and make mistakes." Ugh! Talk about a boring answer! Talk about sounding like a clone of the last 20 people they've interviewed! Talk about sounding so 1990's! A better tactic is saying something to the effect of, "I know the job applicant playbook is to take a take a weakness and reposition it as a positive, however, doing that seems dishonest and doesn't truly help you get a real picture of me."

Then, go on to talk about something that happened many years ago that you learned from like, "When I was a beginner, I remember a time I was struggling with my work and was starting to run late. I did not want anyone to know I was having difficulty so I started to work long and hard on it and was starting to get behind on things. And from this, I learned a great lesson about how what I do has an impact upon others and what they do. Every once in awhile, i get caught up in this same rat hole of being so determined and need a reminder to ask for support."

You have now poked fun of your competitors and their answers while revealing a need for support that may be useful to you and involving your future manager with supporting you.

2. How would you improve the performance of a team and upgrade their standards?

This question is best answered from the viewpoint of performance improvement and development, rather than discipline and control. It's best to interpret this as working to help people become the best that they can be, in ways that enable them to align their natural strengths and preferences with the needs of the organization and the team.

3. **Tell me about a time when you had to plan and coordinate a project from start to finish.**

This is one of the standard behavioral interview questions—a question that is asked to have you explain your experience based upon the bias that past behavior is the best predictor of future performance.

Thus, in advance of your interview take time to carefully construct an answer to this question following the STAR, SOAR or PAR formats for answering interview questions discussed earlier.

4. **Why do you want this job?**

In other words, do you know what you want, and is this job it?

"I've been very careful about the companies that I have tried to interview for positions with. When I heard about this job, I knew I found what I was looking for.

What I can bring to this role is my x years of experience, and knowledge of the industry, plus my ability to communicate and build relationships. That, along with my flexibility and organizational skills, makes me a great match for this position. I see some challenges ahead of me here, and that's what I thrive on. I have what you need, and you have what I want."

5. **What are your salary expectations for this job?**

What salary are you looking for? To translate this from corporate-speak, are you going to be reasonable in your salary demands? Can we afford you?

This question has various ways to answer it. One is,

"I'll need more information about the job and the responsibilities involved before I can answer this question. Can you give me an idea of the range budgeted for this position?" Or

"I'm making x dollars per year plus bonus. Last year, the value of the bonus was $y per year. I'm looking for an opportunity. If you decide I'm the right person for this job, and I certainly think this would be a great opportunity for me, I ask you to make your strongest offer.

Even with the second answer, there is a way to avoid being pinned down to a specific number. You do that by continuing to say, "I am speaking with several other firms that do appear to be interested and it is possible that after I learned more about the position and I hear about the offers from firms I salary expectations may evolve. After all, the market may decide that my value is higher than what I originally believe it to be.

If they challenge you about this, respond by saying,
"Hey look, I'm being honest about this. Most of the time job hunters won't tell you the truth when answering this question. After all, if you thought you are worth $x per year only to discover you are worth $x+20, when your thinking evolve? Of course, it would."

Then, look at them in the eyes and don't say a word.

6.   Why Should I Hire You From the Outsider When I Could Promote Someone Internally?

This is an easy question as long as you don't become defensive. Just remember they already made the decision to hire from the outside before they began interviewing for the job. After all, it would have easier to promote someone, rather than interview you and everyone else, right?

So, give them a bone and then go on to sell. "I don't know the caliber of your team (or the caliber of the internally available candidates). I am sure they are quite able. However, I will speak of my capabilities for this role . . ." Then, go out and sell your ability and your experience as pertains to what they are looking for.

7.   If you had a lot of money, whatever that is for you, tell me three things you would do with it.

The first time I asked this question when screening someone for a sales job, the person I was meeting with told me he would buy a used car and fix it up. This told me that he had set his sites much too low.

The trick to answering this is to make sure the things you choose involve large numbers.

"I would buy a Mercedes sports car, send my parents on the trip to _____ they have always wanted to go on, and with the remaining few hundred thousand, I would invest it in real estate. There are some great opportunities out there!"

8. How do you define success? How do you measure up to your definition?

Offer a well-accepted definition of success that leads right into your collection of achievements and accomplishments.

"Some years ago, I read a definition of success that defined it as the progressive realization of a worthy goal."

"As to how I would measure up to that definition, I would consider myself both successful and fortunate…" (Then summarize your career goals and how your achievements have indeed represented a progressive path toward realization of your goals.)

9. What is your greatest professional strength?

Most people make the mistake of talking way too much or vomiting an answer on the interviewer that is extremely generic that has nothing to do with the position being interviewed for.

They speak about being hardworking. They speak about being a team player or a leader. No one however says, "I am a lazy maverick who would rather follow instructions and get out of doing work."

Telling a story where someone can develop a feeling about you is far better. And it needs to be in the context of the job that you are interviewing for. Describe a situation where your behavior stood out that would benefit the firm you are interviewing for.

For example, you are interviewing for a position as a Director of a function. The firm's profits require improvement (don't they all). You are being asked to reduce costs (don't they all). Fingers are being pointed every which way (don't they always) and people are trying to arrange the deck chairs on a sinking luxury liner.

You paint the picture for the interviewer and then say, "I'm not describing this to be critical. It's just the way it was. I met with a number of my colleagues and encouraged them to make serious plans that involved sacrifice for the benefit of the firm. I offered suggestions and was heard by them. I can foster trust in people because I've earned their trust and respect from my honest dealings with them in the past when a crisis didn't exist."

10. Tell Me About a Mistake You Made

The full question is, "Everyone makes mistakes. I make mistakes. You've made mistakes. Tell me about a (professional) mistake you've made and what you learned from it.

I put the word professional in parentheses because sometimes the question is asked without it and I want to make sure you know that whenever you are asked this question, they are asking you about a professional mistake in judgment.

Do not give them a story of something that happened recently. Recent mistakes can be used to reject your candidacy under the premise that you should have known better than to do what you did.

Instead, try to use a lesson from when you were a beginner . . .and don't sound too rehearsed.

"Hmm! That's a great question." (Pause to think for a minute). "I remember there was a time when I started and was gung ho, I started to fall behind on the project. Instead of letting my manager know that I was struggling, I put in even more effort thinking that through the force of my will, I could turn things around. But I stayed behind what was expected of me and eventually decided to tell my manager. He taught me a great lesson. Everything we do is interdependent. If I struggle, she needs to know because it affects others. Even today, I encourage my people to tell me as soon as they can about problems because their work is connected with other people's work and impacts it."

See what that does? It takes an old story and brings it into the present in a very human way that everyone can understand. Notice how it is similar to how you answer "the weaknesses" question?

11. Why Do You Want to Work Here?

One of my clients uses this question all the time. In their case, they are an internationally known publisher that has a great, well-known brand. Not every company is as well-known as they are.

Do I have to remind you that **before every interview,** take the time to research the firm you are meeting with. What is going on at the firm from a business standpoint? What is your understanding about the job? Then, feed it back to them starting with this line:

Why would I want to work here? Who wouldn't want to work here? This is an opportunity to work for an _____ on such and such where I can help _____! Why wouldn't want someone want to do that!

By letting your enthusiasm out and feeding back what you understand the opportunity to be, you will let them know of your interest (something that employers always want to know) and confirm that you understand the job and the opportunity.

12. Why Have You Been Out of Work So Long?

When the job market is terrible, the answer is pretty easy--I have interviewed at several places but, as you know, the market is extremely competitive and I have finished #2 on several searches.

When the job market is terrific and you represent yourself as having extremely marketable skills and, say, six months later, you're still looking for work, employers look at you differently. They start to ask, "What's wrong with this guy/person/woman that they are still looking for work?"

They really do start to think that there is something wrong, even if the question isn't asked of you. As such, it is important to tell them at some point in the interview that since leaving your last job:

1.   You took time off for a long vacation. You haven't had in eons
2.   You traveled to visit family abroad. You haven't seen them in years.
3.   You took time off to clear your mind after years of work.
4.   You've been taking formal courses in your discipline that you never had time to take before and are now ready to return to work. You've been looking for only a few weeks now (not, say, the full six months you've been out of work).
Unless you say something about this, they will always wonder and when they wonder, they start to look at other alternatives. And when that happens, they never return to you.

13.   What is the Hardest Thing About Being a (Your Job Title)?

Start by re-framing "hardest" into "challenging.".

Then, identify an area everyone in your profession considers challenging and in which you excel. Describe the process you follow that enables you to get results…and be specific about those results. For example, "I think every program manager finds it difficult to coordinate project timelines when staff is located in different countries. This has been one of my strengths."

14.   Have You Ever Needed to Fire Someone?

Firing someone is seen as a failure of the hiring process and management. We made a bad decision. We were not able to successfully motivate someone we believed would do a good job of performing up to their abilities.

Do not make jokes about it.

There are two schools of thought as to how to perform a firing and thus how to answer the question.

Generally, the correct answer in the US is that you documented performance issues and behavioral problems, met with the person privately to counsel and advise them to improve, designated a managerial coach and when that failed, did what was necessary to remove the disappointing employee before their poor performance impacted others and became cancerous.

The other answer was provided at Harvard B-School by the son of an extremely successful industrialist who ran businesses worldwide. His answer was, "Are you kidding me? You take that person into the room and in front of everyone you fire him! You make an example out of that lazy so and so and get rid of him and humiliate him. NO one will ever pull that crap again!"

There are smaller companies and entrepreneurial companies that will love that answer so I want to make sure you hear it and are prepared to offer it if it makes sense for you and the situation you're in.

15. Why Are You Looking (for a Job)?

Too often, people answer this question immaturely. By this, I mean an answer that allows a new employer to interpret the answer as being, "I hate my boss," or "I want to make more money." It is extremely important to:

Keep Your Answers Concise. "Our firm was acquired and management brought in a team that they were familiar with. That's understandable to me but the result was that I was offered assignments that were at a level below where I was with little opportunity to return to my previous level. Rather than remain for the inevitable layoff, I've decided to look for a new position."

Speak positively Do not criticize management for decisions they've made. Do not appear angry. A matter of fact attitude will dispel doubt far better than rage ever will. By looking at the interviewer square in the eyes and preparing your concise answer, most people are persuaded that you are being sincere . . . even though we all know the best liars can look someone square in the eye and lie to us.

Speak about what you learned from this experience. Although this is a tough interview question in itself, anticipate this question and be prepared to speak of the growth opportunity you derived from the experience of the firm. If you made mistakes and can speak to those with sincerity (and without shooting yourself in the foot), firms will see that you are someone who can learn and grow. And sometimes the right answer is to say, "I've thought about my experience with XYZ quite a lot and, the fact is, my performance was always strong. My performance reviews are glowing and managers always found me to be an important contributor. No, I can't say I made mistakes and I was happy to help my firm transition to the new parent company."

REMEMBER: When they ask qualifying follow up questions, just stay with your original answer and state the facts!

16. What Motivates You?

There is no right or wrong answer to this question. It is an opportunity to demonstrate character and leadership that shows you can become a great hire for the firm. In other words, this is an easy question that you can think about and prepare for in advance. So as you prepare for this question, be prepared to discuss some of the challenges you have faced and how you exceeded expectations, offering specific examples in the context of your answer.

If you are in sales, you might say something like, "Having been in commission-based sales throughout my career, I have always been motivated to be the number #1 salesperson earning the top compensation in the firm."

If you are in a role that provides service, you might say: "In my role, I love to help clients receive an extraordinary experience and, through that, help my firm achieve extraordinary success.

If you are in a technology-related job, you might say: I directed development teams on several projects and was responsible for _____. My teams achieved 100% on-time delivery and were motivated by the challenge of finishing the projects ahead of schedule and by managing the teams that achieved our goals."

Then, if you haven't done so already, offer concrete examples of challenging situations where you delivered.

17. How Do You Make Difficult Decisions?

Firms want to believe that the new supervisor they hire is not a lone wolf, a maverick, or a gunslinger.

As a result, they will be listening to hear whether you act alone, in concert with others, asking for advice before you have some ideas or whether you make a decision, and check to see whether it passes a "sniff test" (Oooh! That idea stinks).

The best thing you can do is acknowledge how, when you were young, you acted on your own without a lot of input and learned the lesson that you weren't expected to know everything but expected to make smart decisions. Once you learned that lesson, you learned that it was important to ask great questions and have very good advisers. Always use an example of a difficult decision to illustrate your point!

18. What Would You Do If a Peer (Fellow Manager, Fellow Executive) Was Not Pulling Their Weight?

Try to gauge the style of the firm and be guided accordingly.

In general, fall back on universal principles of effective human relations which, in the end, embody the way you would like to be treated in a similar circumstance.

"Good human relations would call for me to go directly to the person and explain the situation, to try to enlist his or help in a constructive, positive solution. If I sensed resistance, I would be as persuasive as I know how to explain the benefits we can all gain from working together, and the problems we, the company and our customers will experience if we don't."

And what would you do if he still did not change his ways?

"One thing I wouldn't do is let the problem slide because it would only get worse and overlooked and set a bad precedent. I would try again and again and again, in whatever way I could, to solve the problem, involving wider and wider circles of people, both above and below the offending executive, including my boss if necessary, so that everyone involved can see the rewards for teamwork and the drawbacks of non-cooperation."

"I might add that I've never yet come across a situation that couldn't be resolved by harnessing others in a determined, constructive effort."

19. Aren't You Overqualified for This Job?

When a firm asks this question, they are putting the elephant that is standing in the middle of the room squarely into play. They are worried that you will be bored and quit when something better comes along . . . and frankly they are right.

You probably *will* quit because this is probably a job at a lower level than what you have been in and is paying considerably less than what you were earning.

Rather than lie and say, "Oh, no, I want to take a demotion and work for much less than what I was used to earning, try this:

"The job market is a marketplace and like any marketplace, it's subject to the laws of supply and demand. Right now, it's very tight. I understand and accept that. I believe that there could be very positive benefits for both of us in this match because I have a lot of experience in _____ . I can be a strong contributor right away, perhaps much faster than someone who'd have to be brought along more slowly. I can also help you in a lot of ways that many less experienced people can't-- how to hire, train, motivate, even coach, some of the junior people.

"I want to work and, frankly, your position is exactly what I love to do and do extremely well. I'll be happy doing this work and that's what matters most to me, rather than a lot more than money or title. At the same time, I'm looking to make a long term commitment in my career now.

I've had enough of job-hunting and want a permanent position at this juncture in my career. I also know that if I perform well, other opportunities cannot help but open up for me here. "

REMEMBER: Their goal is to figure out if you will be bored and are willing to commit to them. Your answer needs to show that.

20. Sell This to Me (Interviewer Picks Up Something from Their Desk)

The most important secret of all great salesmanship – *"find out what a person wants and show them how to get it."*

If your interviewer picks up his pen and asks, "sell this to me," demonstrate this principle.

"A good salesman must know both his product and his prospect before he sells anything. If I were selling this, I'd first get to know everything I could about it, all its features and benefits."

"Then, if I were to sell it to *you*, I would do some research on how you might use a fine pen like this. The best way to do that is by asking questions. May I ask you a few questions?"

Then ask a few questions such as, "Just out of curiosity, if you didn't already have a pen like this, why would you want one? And in addition to that? Any other reason? Anything else?" "And would you want a pen like this to be reliable?... What color ink, etc..?" (Ask more questions that point to the features this pen has.)

Once you've asked these questions, make your presentation citing all the features and benefits of this pen and why it's exactly what the interviewer just told you he's looking for.

Then close with, "Just out of curiosity, what would you consider a reasonable price for a beautiful writing implement like this...a stapler whatever is,. . . you could have *right now* and would (then repeat all the problems the pen would solve for him)?

Whatever he says, (unless it's zero), say, "Okay, we've got a deal.

Questions You May Want to Ask

During early-round interviews, you want to keep your questions focused on the job in their expectations of you. However, if things keep moving forward and you talk to more people, there is an opportunity for you to ask additional questions so you get a clearer picture of what it is that they're looking for and what it will be like working there.

Here are some questions you might want to ask. Don't ask all of them! Most will not be relevant for the job that you are interviewing for.

But some will be and you will want to ask them at an appropriate time (not with the screener or the first person after that you speak with).

Questions an Early Career Person or Recent Graduate Might Ask

How long do people usually stay in this role?

Why did the last person leave this job?

Please explain your organizational structure to me? Where does this position fit in? How many people work in this department?

How long have you worked here?

Why do people leave?

What are the company's strengths and weaknesses as compared to the competition?

What is the vision of the company?

What are the best opportunities in your company for new hires like me?

Are there major changes in the industry occurring and how is the company responding?

What would you consider to be the most important aspects of this job?

Questions Experienced Professionals Might Want to Ask

What do you see as your company's strengths and weaknesses compared to its competition?

How do you see the future for this industry?

How important does senior management consider the function of this department and position?
What is the best thing about working for the company? What does the company pride itself on? What is the organization's plan for the next five years and how do this department and job fit into those plans?

Please explain your org structure to me and how I would fit in.

What do you consider to be your firm's most important assets?

What can you tell me about your new product or your growth plans?

How do you rate your competition?

What happened to the last person who held this job? What were the major strengths and weaknesses of the last person who held this job?

Thinking back to the person who you've seen do this job best, what made their performance so outstanding?

What types of skills do you NOT already have onboard that you're looking to fill with a new hire?

Please describe a typical workday or workweek.

Please describe the typical colleague, client, and/or customer I would be dealing with?

Who do you enjoy working with the most here? What is it about them that you enjoy?

What are the skills and attributes you value most for someone being hired for this position?

What possibilities will exist for me to learn new things? What might I become involved with that I don't already know?

What is the company's policy on providing seminars, workshops, and training so employees can keep up their skills or acquire new ones?

What technology will I be working with? What are the most immediate challenges of the position that need to be addressed in the first three months? How often will I be reviewed and based upon what criteria?

What rewards exist for someone who outperforms their peers?

How would you describe the culture here?

How would you describe your management style?

Jeff Altman

The Big Game Hunter

J eff Altman, The Big Game Hunter is a coach who worked as a recruiter for what seems like one hundred years. His work involves career coaching, all as well as executive job search coaching, job coaching, and interview coaching. He is the host of "No BS Job Search Advice Radio," the #1 podcast in iTunes for job search with more episodes than any other show by more than 2:1, a top-rated YouTube channel at JobSearchTV.com plus an OTT television channel available through the Job Search TV app for Amazon and Roku, as well as through BingeNetworks.tv for AppleTV and 90+ smart tv platforms. He is also a member of The Forbes Coaches Council.

If you are interested in 1:1 coaching, interview coaching, advice about networking more effectively, how to negotiate your offer or leadership coaching? Schedule a free discovery call or coaching session at The Big Game Hunter.us

If you have a quick question for me, you can get it answered with a 3-5 minute video at

www.TheBigGameHunter.us/videoanswer.

Want to do speak with me live?

Book 15 minutes at www.TheBigGameHunter.us/live

Connect with me on LinkedIn at

www.linkedin.com/in/TheBigGameHunter

You can order a copy of "Diagnosing Your Job Search Problems" for Kindle on Amazon and receive free Kindle versions of "No BS Resume Advice" and "Interview Preparation."

If you are starting your search, order, "Get Ready for the Job Jungle."

www.ingramcontent.com/pod-product-compliance
Lightning Source LLC
Chambersburg PA
CBHW071030220526
45467CB00004B/1596